This book will be a ... Christians who ex... those who seek to help ... combination of Biblical principles, medical knowledge and pastoral wisdom.

Vaughan Roberts
Rector of St Ebbe's Oxford
And Director of Proclamation Trust
Oxford

Dealing with Depression is a helpful work both for those struggling with depression and for those helping someone who is suffering through debilitating despair. Sarah Collins and Jayne Haynes offer a realistic biblical view of depression that acknowledges the tension between the weaknesses brought about by the Fall and the faithfulness of God in and through suffering. Personal testimonies at the end of each chapter were especially helpful in articulating the nuances of both the struggle and the journey associated with depression. I encourage every church leader and member to read this booklet so that they will see how the gospel feeds the soul, enflames hope, and enables perseverance in the darkness of life, all through the grace of Christ.

Robert K. Cheong
Pastor of Care and Counseling
Sojourn Community Church
Louisville, Kentucky

Sensitive, informative, insightful, biblical, pastoral and practical, this book will be of help both to those who experience depression and those seeking to help those suffering with depression.

Jonathan Prime
Pastor of Enfield Evangelical Free Church
London

Dealing with Depression

Trusting God
through the Dark Times

SARAH COLLINS AND JAYNE HAYNES

Copyright © Sarah Collins and Jayne Haynes 2011

paperback ISBN 978-1-84550-633-9
epub ISBN 978-1-84550-997-2
mobi ISBN 978-1-84550-796-1

10 9 8 7 6 5 4 3

Published in 2011
Reprinted in 2012 & 2015
by
Christian Focus Publications,
Geanies House, Fearn,
Ross-shire, IV20 1TW, Scotland, United Kingdom
www.christianfocus.com

Cover design
by Dufi-art.com

Printed and bound by
Nørhaven, Denmark

CONTENTS

Acknowledgments

We are very grateful indeed to Roger Carswell, Julian Hardyman, Al Horn, Anne Norrie, Vaughan Roberts, Andrew Sach, and Ed Shaw for their help, wisdom and support in putting this book together. We would also like to thank all the anonymous contributors who were happy to write down their 'stories' for us to share in this book. Thanks too to our wonderful husbands and children for bearing with us during the writing of it.

Preface

Depression is one of the major health challenges of our generation, particularly in the developed world. Christians are not immune from it. Our aim in writing this short book is to equip the friends, families and church families of those suffering from depression to better help them. We hope that the mix of biblical truths, pastoral advice and medical information in this book will help readers to offer practical advice and support grounded in biblical principles to those suffering with depression. We hope that readers struggling with depression themselves may also find the book helpful – but please bear with us that this is not intended to be a self-help book – more a source of information.

We first began thinking in depth about the issue of depression and the Christian when we became aware of how many of our own church family were battling with depression. With backgrounds in Christian student work (Sarah) and family medicine (Jayne) we put together a seminar on the topic, and eventually this has evolved into this booklet. This is far from being a comprehensive book, but we hope and pray that you will find it a useful introduction to this topic. Needless to say it probably won't match every person's experience and certainly won't be able to give a full picture of depression in all its complexity. Our hope is that it will give a bit of a handle on the subject for those who don't know much about it who may be helping others suffering with depression or suffering themselves.

We have written primarily for Christians and we will try to understand depression from both a medical and Biblical perspective. But since Jesus is Lord over every human being, we hope it will have relevance too for those who haven't yet come to know Him for themselves.

Depression: What is it?

1

Depression:

What is it?

The medical term depression refers to a range of mental health conditions with a common thread of persistent low mood. Depression is fast becoming one of the most common complaints people take to the doctor's surgery. Currently depression is the third most common reason to consult a family doctor in the UK and it is estimated that approximately 15 per cent of people in the UK will have at least one episode of major depression in their life time – and that's just those who are actually diagnosed by a doctor.[1] Many more will have milder

---

1 Clinical Knowledge Summaries. Depression. http://www.cks.nhs.uk/depression/background_information/prevalence [last accessed 1 March 2011].

episodes of depression. The World Health Organisation has predicted it will be 'the most disabling condition of the twenty-first Century' having a significant impact on the workplace as sufferers take time off, and on families of sufferers who bear a great deal of the strain. The economic costs are enormous, estimated at over £9 billion each year in England alone.[2] Although it often has physical causes and effects, it is primarily an illness of the mind, and its frequency has caused doctors to speak of it as 'the common cold of the mind'. It is difficult to say whether it is more common now than it was in times gone by. Certainly people have always suffered with it, even if it went under different names such as 'melancholy'. Perhaps it is more readily diagnosed now, or perhaps it is a consequence to be expected from living increasingly fast and stressful lives, in an increasingly broken and insecure society. Whilst its prevalence may lead to comparison with the common cold, that is about as far as the similarities between

2   Thomas CM and Morris S. *Cost of Depression in England in 2000*. British Journal of Psychiatry 2003;183:514-9.

depression and the common cold go. Depression is a significant health problem and a long way from some sneezing and a runny nose, which for most of us is a relatively trivial affair.

FEELING DEPRESSED OR GOT 'DEPRESSION'?

People often ask, 'What's the difference between depression and feeling unhappy?' Clearly we all have times in our lives when we feel down for all kinds of reasons and we may even say we 'feel depressed'. It is important to distinguish here between 'feeling depressed' and 'having Depression' with a capital D, as it were (by which we are speaking of those diagnosed by a doctor as having clinical depression).

It may help to imagine our emotions are on a spectrum ranging from 'Definitely not depressed' to 'Definitely depressed'. We can all move up and down this spectrum at different times in our lives, even in the course of a day!

Definitely not depressed	Definitely depressed
<-->	

When trying to decide whether or not someone has depression a doctor will consider what symptoms they have and compare this to various criteria that have been developed by experts.[3] Often a doctor might encourage a patient to complete various questionnaire tools to help the doctor and patient to work together to decide whether or not the patient has clinical depression. It is almost as though there is a cut-off point along our spectrum between definitely not depressed and definitely depressed – a cut-off which marks the difference between feeling low and having clinical depression, and someone who meets the 'expert criteria' for depression will be on the 'definitely depressed' side of that cut-off.

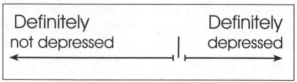

The cut-off is a bit of a simplification: it is possible to be very close to it, or to fluctuate backwards and forwards over it, and

---

3   e.g. ICD-10 (International Classification of Diseases) http://www.who.int/classifications/icd/en/ [last accessed 1 March 2011].

even within a diagnosis of depression there are varying degrees of severity; indeed someone with severe depression may well feel that their emotions are in a completely different league to anything they have experienced before.

What is helpful about seeing our emotions on a spectrum is that it shows that the depressed person is not in a whole separate category from the rest of us. It can be tempting when we hear that someone has depression, to see them as if they are in a box and to assume that they can't or won't get out of it. Realising they are just a bit further (or sometimes quite a lot further) down the emotional spectrum than the average person helps us to remember that they can also move back towards the healthy end of the spectrum given time and the right help. Just as we all move up and down a spectrum of physical health, going through times of good health and times of bad health, so it is with our emotional health, and recovery in most cases is not only possible, but normal.

Having said that, because depression is in one sense just a very severe form of feeling unhappy, it may be tempting to apply the usual kind of 'pull yourself together!' or 'cheer up!' advice to someone suffering with it. It is vital to understand that when a person gets that far towards the end of the spectrum there is no simple 'snapping out' of it. Just as when a person becomes severely physically ill, they can't be expected to get better 'just like that' or without help, so it is with the person suffering with the illness of depression. Indeed this may be even more the case with depression than with a purely physical illness – because at least with a purely physical illness sufferers are able to think clearly about the situation whereas in times of depression it can be very difficult to get a clear perspective on the problem and to reason with oneself about the situation.

SIGNS AND SYMPTOMS OF DEPRESSION

We all have times of feeling low and unhappy, but when a person is suffering from depression these feelings are stronger and the times go on for longer than life's normal ups and downs.

Symptoms that might clearly point to depression include feeling low or sad most of the day and losing interest in life.

Other things that may point to depression include:

- Anxiety or panic problems
- Loss of appetite or weight
- Difficulty thinking clearly – perhaps including poor concentration and difficulty making decisions
- Not coping with things that normally would be manageable
- Feeling tired all the time
- Sleep problems – ranging from not being able to get to sleep, to waking early in the morning, to sleeping too much
- Feeling worthless or guilty
- Recurrent thoughts of death and dying, possibly including thoughts about suicide
- Irritability or anger
- Feeling restless or agitated
- Crying easily
- Introspection
- Over-sensitivity or heightened paranoia
- Seeing everything through a negative filter
- Feeling hopeless about the future

- Avoiding being with other people
- Aches and pains that do not have another cause – for example headaches, muscle aches and bowel symptoms.

From a pastoral point of view, it may be helpful when trying to distinguish between depression and life's normal ups and downs to consider whether the symptoms are preventing someone from functioning normally and how long they have had the symptoms for. It is very likely that someone with depression will find that their symptoms have been present for some time and that they interfere with everyday life.

TIME TO SEE A DOCTOR?

Many people suffering from mild depression won't need to see a doctor – although a family doctor will always be happy to help people concerned that they might be depressed. It is not uncommon for people who have depression to be reluctant to seek medical help – for all sorts of reasons. For people who have initially tried to manage their depression without the help of a health professional, indications that it might be time to see a family doctor or a counsellor include:

- the symptoms being severe
- the symptoms having gone on for a long time
- not making much progress with approaches such as self-help and pastoral support
- thoughts of suicide

Another reason for encouraging someone who might have depression to see a doctor is that we should allow the diagnosis of depression to be made by a health professional – and avoid the temptation of making the diagnosis ourselves – an incorrect label of depression can be just as harmful as refusing to acknowledge a genuine problem with depression.

ANN'S STORY (21, STUDENT)

In my experience depression is a bit like walls closing in so that it's difficult to see beyond the perceived walls to the realities and people around you. Losing perspective like that means relational and practical things become stressful, and this can build up to become extremely disabling and confusing. At one point I was in such despair I would shut down completely if asked to do anything but sit in my room.

Spiritually I felt at first that God was punishing me for being insecure and proud rather than finding my security in him. This meant it was really hard to turn to him for comfort and help, but in time I saw this was a wrong view of grace and depression. I now think depression is God's way of helping me find security in him, as the painful experience brought to the surface lots of repressed anger and bitterness, and the many ways I've developed to cover up and protect myself. It prevents self-reliance and gives a hunger for God that is harder to cultivate in easier times.

Without an understanding of depression it was very difficult to be nourished by the Bible and to pray, to relate considerately to other Christians, or to live as a Christian in the world. I felt difficulties were choking me spiritually. Listening to sermons and the prayers of others became acutely painful, as the many challenges left me feeling overwhelmed and useless, seeing only the negative rather than a God of grace. I often used to leave church meetings in an even greater sense of hopelessness. But teaching and fellowship from church really helped me accept and, in time, recover from depression.

Medication, pastoral care, counselling, friends and a structured lifestyle have also been a great help. Someone said to me that love and work are the best cures to depression, and it's wonderful how God provides relationship and purpose in so many different ways. Experiencing the Lord's compassion during depression caused much change in me, and it is certainly something God has used to keep me and ensure I enjoy him more both in this life and the next.

CATHERINE'S STORY (36, UNIVERSITY LECTURER)

Looking back it's hard now to remember what the depths of depression really felt like. Except to say it's rather like having a stomach bug: feeling pretty constantly grim, peppered by regular bouts of sickness. Only the tidal waves of emotional sickness aren't a result of a dodgy prawn sandwich but are waves of utter despair – for no reason, and yet for every reason – because everything is wrong.

Depression is often said to be like the common cold of mental illness – in that it's so common, or like a broken arm – in that you shouldn't hesitate to accept treatment. Of course it is like any other ailment. And yet it isn't at all: it's like a battle raging in your mind, a mind which normally you have control over. It's is also very different from feeling low; it's not just at the extreme end of regular emotions. It's just not on the scale at all.

I found antidepressants took a while to make a difference, but they really did, giving me control over my thoughts again and I'm very well now. But I'm not the same person that I was before – just a little bit less at ease with life, just a little bit less able to cope with change and uncertainty, just a little bit more sensitive.

Three things spring to mind that God used to help me keep going during the darkest days: friends and family whose love and care – and time – made Proverbs 17:17 come to life; good quality Christian hymns, new and old, that spoke truth to my troubled soul; and the hope of Revelation 21 when everything will be made new and perfect.

Why do people get depressed?

2

Why do people get depressed?

The medical causes of depression are not fully understood. Like many illnesses it seems that there are multiple inter-related factors that influence whether or not an individual will be vulnerable to depression. For many people there will be a combination of a background predisposition to developing the illness coupled with some precipitating factor(s) that finally tips a person into an episode of depression. Major depression is an illness and the person should not blame themselves, or be blamed by others, for suffering from it.

- Biology – it is widely accepted that an imbalance in various chemicals in the brain can cause depression. It also seems that some medical conditions such as strokes, Parkinson's disease and thyroid problems may cause depression.

- Circumstances – someone's circumstances both past and present may make them vulnerable to depression. For example traumatic life events such as bereavement, relationship breakdown or job loss may contribute to a person developing depression. Different people find different things difficult – so there are as many different situations that may make someone vulnerable to depression as there are people. Common situations that might make someone vulnerable to depression include being socially isolated, being 'burnt out', or being unhappy at work or at home.

DEPRESSION IN PARTICULAR SITUATIONS

- ### POSTNATAL DEPRESSION

Postnatal depression is a depression that follows the birth of a baby – it is surprisingly common, affecting as many as one in ten new mothers. It usually begins in the first month or so after the baby is born, but may come on several months later. Lots of factors may contribute to the depression, and sometimes it is hard to distinguish from the exhaustion of life with a small baby. On top of this mothers may feel guilty that they are not enjoying motherhood as much as they think they should be – and so may be reluctant to admit they are feeling low. As well as the usual strategies for tackling depression, other things that can be helpful with postnatal depression are support from health visitors and practical support from friends and family including making sure new mothers get enough rest and some time for themselves.[1]

• DEPRESSION AND YOUNG PEOPLE
Depression is not just an illness affecting adults. The symptoms of depression in children and teenagers are largely the same as those in adults; irritability is a common symptom in children and mood can be quite variable in depressed children – sometimes with rapid mood swings. Behaviours that might raise concerns that

1   See Alie Stibbe's book in Resources

a child is suffering from depression include running away from home, self-harming, problems at school (such as refusing to go to school or poor performance at school) and anti-social behaviour. Some groups of young people appear to be particularly vulnerable to depression – for example those who are victims of bullying or other forms of abuse, as well as children who are refugees or living in institutions.

• GRIEF

To feel depressed and display many of the symptoms associated with depression is entirely normal when a person is bereaved or dealing with grief over the loss of someone or something significant in their lives. Bouts of mild to severe depression are a normal part of the grieving process (as well as shock, overwhelming emotion, guilt, anger, preoccupation with the loss and eventually adapting to reality) but these are usually mixed in with periods of normal functioning. A doctor will therefore probably not diagnose this as clinical depression unless the bouts of depressive symptoms give way to a longer period of depression and the sadness is not receding as the person begins to come to terms with the loss. When a person is grieving they will generally respond well to the support of people who care and, unlike many depressed people, won't tend to shun social contact. Grief is certainly more socially acceptable – there is a specific cause and others are more able to empathise and care for those grieving (especially since it is generally for a more limited period of time). Depressed people often feel (and are) more isolated, less understood and more difficult to help. People who are already depressed and then experience grief are particularly vulnerable as they often don't have the resources to deal with this and those around them need to be doubly concerned to give them care and support.

• ANXIETY
Anxiety and depression often come to-gether, and sometimes it can be difficult to work out which is the main problem. Whilst it is normal to feel anxious in certain situations, it is not uncommon for depressed people to feel unduly anxious. Many of the treatments for depression discussed later can also help with anxiety.

- MANIC DEPRESSION – ALSO KNOWN AS
  BIPOLAR DISORDER

Up to one in ten individuals with severe clinical depression may be suffering from manic depression. This is an illness where sufferers not only experience the intense lows of severe depression, but also extreme highs of mania. Mania is an extremely elevated mood, and may include reckless behaviours such as spending vast amounts of money, being extremely busy doing things and having an inflated self-esteem. Manic depression usually requires specialist help from a psychiatrist but with their help and the right medication can be brought under control. More information about bipolar disorder can be found at the Royal College of Psychiatrists website[2].

- BORDERLINE PERSONALITY DISORDER
  (BPD)

BPD is a mental health problem that is largely about instability in relationships with other people, often with a fear of rejection and with problems around low self-image and low mood. Impulsive behaviour including self-harm (for example superficial cuts

---

2   See Resources appendix

to the wrists, or taking an overdose of tablets) can also be a feature. Sufferers may become unhelpfully dependent on other people. People with BPD are vulnerable to developing depression – and will often benefit from many of the strategies used to treat depression, however sometimes different approaches from those used for depression may be more helpful. More information about personality disorders can be found on the Royal College of Psychiatrists website.

COMMON MISCONCEPTIONS

ABOUT DEPRESSION

In pondering the causes of depression we come across some very murky waters – human emotion is hard for anyone to understand. To add to the confusion, the causes for each person will, to some extent, be unique to that person and their particular physical, emotional, spiritual, mental and social make-up. It may be easier to identify errors and over-simplifications in people's understanding of where depression comes from, than to attempt to give any clear answers. And so here are two errors which we Christians are especially prone to make in trying to understand the causes of depression:

• ERROR 1: DEPRESSION IS PURELY SPIRITUAL
The first error is to assume that the problem of depression is entirely a spiritual matter. We may perhaps think it must be a reflection on the depressed person's inadequate spiritual life, a failure to really trust God or perhaps some unconfessed sinful attitude or behaviour. It is true that in some cases there are spiritual and sinful factors that contribute to a person's depression, and it is undoubtedly the case that all depressed believers will have spiritual challenges to face and ways in which the Lord wants them to grow through their experience. But it is simply not the case that the cause of every person's depression is a particular sin. The Bible gives us many examples of believers who were very low, sometimes to the point of not wanting to live, and yet the cause is not identified as sin in their lives. Their emotional struggles are related to difficult circumstances such as loss, persecution, exile, pressure, isolation, for example, Job, Elijah, (1 Kings 19) and many of the psalmists (as we shall explore in more depth in chapter 5). Some-

times we aren't told much of the specific circumstances, the focus is more on the overwhelming sorrow that has all but got the better of them. And this sorrow (and often even the accompanying doubt and anger) is not condemned as being a failure to trust God, but rather contained within the experience of people who are trusting in God. Suffice to say that to always assume a sinful cause to a person's depression is to misunderstand the Bible's portrayal of our human frailty as well as to ignore the medical aspect of depression as an illness of the mind. Such an attitude is at best unhelpful and misguided, at worst, deeply cruel and judgmental.

• ERROR 2: DEPRESSION IS PURELY MEDICAL This second error is to uncritically absorb the kinds of views we might hear in the world around us that belong more to the spirit of our age than to the Bible. It is to leave spiritual questions out of our understanding of depression and to assume that depression is a purely medical problem. This might lead us to assume that in every case those who suffer with it are victims of the illness, they cannot help it, they just have to go with it.

There is truth in all this, but it is a truth that varies as much as every individual who is depressed. We are all responsible before God as much as we are victims of living in an imperfect world where life can really hurt. For some who suffer depression it may be the case that a significant part of it is their own responsibility.

This was certainly true for David in Psalm 32. He spoke of his groaning, his bones wasting away, his strength sapped, of God's hand being 'heavy' upon him. The reason was some unspecified sin and the solution was repentance. There are some believers who would also testify to this experience in their own lives, as if their depression were like God's loving hand of discipline laying heavy on them. In such cases God convicts of specific sin to turn from – perhaps an ungodly attitude such as an unwillingness to forgive, making an idol of someone or something else, bitterness or all-consuming self-pity. Or perhaps it is some sinful behaviour such as an addiction or a wrong relationship.

We all struggle with these kinds of things, but occasionally God will graciously bring us very low indeed and use the discipline of depression to loosen the grip of these things and show us again that our lives belong to him and that he is worthy of our complete trust and obedience. Depression can be an opportunity for serious heart searching for the Christian believer. If there is specific sin God will show us as we ask him to do so (and it may also be helpful to talk to one or two mature Christians for their honest observations rather than trusting our own diagnosis in this). But even if there is no specific sinful cause, which is often the case, it is a time to remember again God's faithfulness and renew our dependence on him and grow in trust of him through the trial.

Hannah's story (27, administrator)

Over the last seven years I've had an ongoing 'battle' with clinical depression that has been an up and down process with three serious lows each lasting between six months to a year. During the worst patches, my life is massively affected by the illness: sleeping fourteen hours solid each night obviously leaves less day-time; lack of energy and motivation make it hard to 'achieve' much when I am awake. Difficulty interacting with other people (partly, at least, because of an excessive and highly critical self-awareness) can prevent me leaving the house, and a grim sense of hopelessness undermines my usual positivity. All these factors combine to make day-to-day life horrid. This has led to being unable to socialise or work, a patch in hospital and many months of being cared for by my parents.

Whilst I always know that I am just one whole person, the nature of this process can make it seem that over time there are two different 'Hannahs' battling for the role of 'being me' – a positive, motivated, confident, smiley, energetic person (the one I like to think of myself as really being…!) and a despairing, self-hating, suicidal person who knows she can't cope. And I guess this points to one of the areas I think God is lovingly working at through all this messyness – He wants to teach me to rely on Him and not myself and He knows that by allowing me to experience such loss of all 'my ability' I can do nothing else.

Although I rarely find myself doubting the facts of the Christian faith, when I'm really poorly I sometimes find it very difficult to feel the reality of God's love for me in Jesus or hang onto the hope He has given me for the future and His grace to me in the present. I am gradually learning to trust that the relationship between God and myself is dependent on Him and not on how I'm feeling. God is in control of my health and He's using its frailty to keep me trusting and growing in humble dependence on Him.

I am so grateful for His provision of support and encouragement through a women's Bible study group, great books (Gaius Davies' *Genius, Grief and Grace* has helped me hugely), healthcare (both medication and Cognitive Behavioural Therapy) and my family and friends. It's not much fun for them seeing the desperation, introversion and exhaustion and yet God has also used these struggles to work in and through them.

Medical treatments for depression and a Christian perspective on them

3

Medical Treatments for depression and a Christian perspective on them

Four out of five people who have depression will get better without any medical help, although this may take many months.

The mainstays of medical treatment for depression are:

- Self-help
- 'Talking treatments'
- Medication

Often more than one of these strategies is employed. It is our opinion that Christians struggling with depression should be encouraged to use all the resources that God has provided – so as well as the Bible, prayer and the support of other Christians we should make use of the conventional medical and psychological treatments that are available.

SELF-HELP

This refers to a depressed person using books and other resources (such as websites) that have been written to help someone with depression understand their illness and develop ways of coping with it. A list of resources is given in the appendix on further reading. Various organisations offer self-help groups where people can get support from others battling with depression.

Unfortunately the very nature of depression means that sometimes self-help feels just too difficult. One strategy that might help at these times is to get help from a supportive friend – perhaps reading the book (or parts of it – they can be quite fat books!) and then meeting to discuss it. Also in this category are practical 'common sense' strategies that might help – such as getting enough sleep and exercise, eating well, and not drinking too much alcohol.

Occasionally secular self-help manuals may promote ideas that Bible-believing Christians may disagree with – most commonly this might be along the lines of 'whatever makes you happy is good'. Our recommendations for using self-help materials would be to consider using a specifically Christian self-help book[1], or to use a good secular book but to be testing it against Bible truths (this may need the help of a Christian friend supporting the depressed person).

TALKING TREATMENTS

This is a cover-all term for the many different 'psychological therapies' that are available – the common ones include counselling, cognitive behavioural therapy (CBT) and psychodynamic psychotherapies. The therapy is given by a trained therapist who will often use a combination of techniques, either in a one–to–one setting, or in a group, for a course of sessions. Computerised CBT is also available online. In the UK talking treatments are available from the National Health Service (NHS) (often accessed through a family doctor), charities and private therapists. CBT in particular has been shown in research to be a good treatment for depression. In

---

1   See appendix

addition to helping with the current episode of depression talking treatments may help people develop strategies for avoiding another attack in the future.

As with self-help there may be times when a secular therapist holds to non-biblical views. However more often than not Christians have lots to gain from talking treatment with a well-trained therapist. We would suggest either using a secular therapist but arranging 'debriefing' sessions with a supportive Christian friend to consider the content of the therapy in the light of the Bible, or alternatively using a Christian therapist. Kirsten Birkett's *The Essence of Psychology* provides more information about the field of psychology and psychological treatments from a Christian perspective.

MEDICATIONS
Antidepressant medications work well for lots of people. They work by altering the levels of chemicals in the brain. There are lots of different types – some work better for some people than others, and the side effects vary between types. In most cases it will take a couple of weeks

for the medication to start to work (and sometimes the depression may get worse before it gets better). If the medication works it is wise to continue it for several months, if the first one doesn't seem to help then it is often worth trying a different one. Antidepressants are available from a family doctor.

Medication is particularly helpful in severe depression – especially when someone is too depressed to try self-help or talking treatments. Once some improvement has occurred, a combination of medication and perhaps CBT can be a good approach. There are some herbal remedies such as St John's Wort, which may help depression.

ECT (Electro-convulsive therapy) may be helpful in severe depression when other treatments have not worked. It involves passing an electric current through the brain to cause a brief seizure.

We do not think there are any specific concerns for Christians considering using antidepressant medication or ECT. If a doctor has recommended it we would strongly support at least trying medication to see if it helps.

SIMON'S STORY (29, TEACHER)

A few years ago I got depressed for no clear reason. I just loathed myself. I was part of a prayer group at the time, and they were a great support, but I had swallowed the lie about self-worth (i.e. that I had none). Sleep and appetite suffered. I don't really recall how or when I got past this, but I was OK again for a time.

The next (and by far the worst) depression was a couple of years later. There were still residual self worth problems; I wasn't cooking for myself, tidying up (I just didn't care about living in a pigsty) or working properly. I couldn't deal with difficult classes; I just gave up.

The final straw was, perhaps predictably, a girl.

Eventually I went to the family doctor and got some medication. This helped a lot; I felt less clouded and able to think. I could see some hope ahead, see possible solutions, and could accept that things could improve.

I still get down, still sometimes feel worthless, still obsess about things, but I can usually take it back to God and wait it out. Sometimes it seems that we can only really expect lasting happiness in heaven, not before. It seems that bad times have a right to be there and that anything else is an aberration. I remember walking through a shopping centre and being hit with a feeling of depression, =ut of nowhere. I've learned to cope; I sat down and just waited, not letting my thoughts get out of hand, and it left. For me, I think that there is a major chemical imbalance aspect to my state, and I need to avoid things that exacerbate this.

The things that have helped have been Christian friends giving time (and hospitality), awareness of the problem, and medication. The experience has helped me be of some use to others who have been in this position. In fact, soon after the worst bout I was able to help a friend who was depressed. Ultimately I trust God knows what He is doing.

Depression and
the Christian

4

Depression and
the Christian

Depressed Christians:

a contradiction in terms?

Some may be tempted to think of it as a contradiction in terms, but genuine Christians do get depressed. Many well known and greatly used Christians throughout history suffered with severe episodes of depression: CS Lewis, Charles Simeon, Martin Luther, Amy Carmichael, William Cowper and many more. And several Bible characters at times displayed symptoms associated with depression: Elijah, Job, Moses, David and many other psalmists. Feeling low didn't mean they weren't believing any more, in fact we see great faith in the way they were looking to God in the midst of emotional turmoil. We often think of depression or feeling low as a weakness. Indeed, it certainly is about being weak, just like getting flu or cancer or a broken leg is about being weak. Because of the Fall we are all physically weak: we get ill and eventually die. Similarly, we are all emotionally weak and get low, sometimes really low. This is just normal human experience and Christians are not immune from it. Life comes with its sickness and its sorrow and we mustn't assume depression is in itself a sin. It stems from living in a sinful world but it isn't necessarily the direct result of some sinful attitude or behaviour in the depressed person.

THE EXPERIENCE OF THE DEPRESSED BELIEVER

On top of the various mental, emotional, physical and behavioural symptoms we have already seen that a depressed person might be dealing with, Christians will have a whole set of spiritual issues to deal with as well. It is common, for example for a depressed believer to feel a deep sense of having been abandoned by God. It is a very dark and confusing time and it is almost inevitable that they will doubt whether God really is there, really loves them and really is for them.

They may also doubt God's power to change them or their circumstances. The future will look pretty bleak most of the time, and their troubles so insurmountable it is easy to forget God is still in control and promises to work for good through all things.

They are unlikely to be experiencing any joy in Christ other than perhaps a vague intellectual assent to the truths that give us reason to rejoice. Lack of joy can cause believers to seriously doubt the authenticity of their faith. This lack of assurance can make spiritual disciplines like reading the Bible and prayer all the more challenging. In such instances a change of expectations can help, for example rather than aiming for in-depth Bible study every day, simply reading through a psalm might be a more realistic aim and praying short, honest prayers.

The depressed believer is likely to feel a great deal of guilt, not only for sin but also for simply being depressed in the first place. This can also be perpetuated by feelings of guilt for not having physical or emotional energy and enthusiasm either in spiritual disciplines or in being as active as they once were (at home, work or church). Guilt is a very common feature in depression for non-Christians, but for the Christian it can take on a new power because we know and speak of our objective guilt before God (apart from in Christ). It may seem like the Bible is just confirming what they feel – that they are guilty and useless, without a hope and beyond the reach of God's grace. Such distortion of the gospel can be clung to by even the most 'mature' of depressed Christians, and many find they seem unable to move from guilt to grace in Christ, unable to trust that He has done it all and they have nothing to prove.

These are huge and painful (albeit, as many would testify, often deeply helpful) battles to face, and with very weak defences. Furthermore, our enemy the Devil prowls around all of us and attacks believers by feeding us lies which can undermine our faith. He might, for example, be telling us that we feel like this because we are beyond hope and that God cannot possibly love us. Those who are depressed can be so vulnerable to his attacks. This is where the church family plays an absolutely vital role which we will look at later.

GOD CAN COPE WITH DEPRESSION

Depression carries a stigma. In our own western culture we are generally fearful of extreme emotion and perceived weakness. This kind of thinking has inevitably infiltrated our thinking as Christians too. The good news is that depression doesn't carry a stigma with God. He 'knows how we are formed and remembers that we are dust' (Ps. 103:13-14). He knows we are mortal even if we like to think we are super human. And his response is compassion. This wonderful word speaks of his complete understanding and unfailing care. The Bible gives us great examples of those who found him to be perfectly compassionate in their times of weakness.

God is also able to use experiences of depression for the good of those who love him (Rom. 8:28-29). Depressed believers often feel they have reached the end of themselves and are acutely conscious of their weakness and utter dependence on God.

This can actually be a very healthy place to be spiritually, if understood in the light of God's grace. Indeed it is far more healthy than the self-sufficiency and pride that we are often guilty of when life seems fine. So depression can be a time of deep and painful learning, but many would testify to the long-term fruit of having understood more of God's sufficient grace and perfect power to keep us in our weakness.

Such experiences may also be used to bless others. It is often those who have struggled with depression who can be some of the most compassionate people in the church, able to empathise with others struggling and offer godly wisdom and practical support in comforting others. [1]

Plenty of Christians who have suffered depression have also been able to express themselves with a creativity that has been a huge blessing to the church. People such as CS Lewis, John Bunyan, Amy Carmichael, and William Cowper have been greatly used in providing the church with books and hymns which express profound truths about God and their need for him.

---

1   See Jo Swinney's book in Resources

Jane's story (55, minister's wife, mother, teacher)
Depression and fear came very unexpectedly, like a thief in the night stripping me bare. For me depression was in a different league to any pain I had previously known.

I felt that I was being asked to endure something beyond my capability. I just didn't know how long I could keep going. In losing my mind I felt I had lost absolutely everything. It was so bad that I was convinced I was beyond healing. Death seemed the only way out. I repeatedly asked Jesus to take me. I had to dig very very deep within my soul to find the courage to keep going, a courage that I didn't know I had.

I had no appetite, I didn't sleep, my body shook uncontrollably and my eyesight was affected. I couldn't concentrate, my body smelled differently. I was paranoid in case people saw me the way I was. I couldn't even get myself to the doctor's on my own. Getting out of bed was like climbing Everest. Keeping clean was an immense effort.

During this time I never lost my faith in God but how I questioned Him. What was He doing to me? I felt this keenly since prayer, my own and others' for me, did not appear to help. Sometimes all I could do was repeat the Lord's Prayer over and over again in my head and out loud. I pleaded with God to heal me, and I know He heard my cries. After months of mental torture I agreed to go in to hospital. I was in hospital for three months.

I didn't respond to any of the medications that were given to me and had to endure the after affects of some of them. But most people do respond to medication or talking therapy and I would urge people not to be afraid of taking medication. I agreed after that to try ECT.

Every day of my life I thank God for the ECT treatment I received. I thank God for the knowledge of the medical staff who delivered it to me. They handed me a life-line which I fearfully grabbed with both hands. I had a total of eight sessions.

The depression started to lift and slowly and steadily I inched myself with God's help out of the pit. I was blessed by receiving help from Mrs R, a Clinical Psychologist. It took time and a lot of perseverance but healing came. I had to engage in physiotherapy of the mind. Today I am medication-free.

Healthy eating, regular exercise and walks, establishing achievable daily routines, making time for myself and time for my husband and keeping to sensible sleeping routines all played a part in my recovery. I read many books to help me. The Psalms were very special to me in my time of recovery. But more than anything it was the love of God, my dear husband and precious family and my wonderful supportive friends who led me out.

Trusting God
in the darkness:
Help from the
Psalmists

5

Trusting God
in the darkness:

Help from the Psalmists

GROANING BEFORE THE LORD

Many Christians who have experienced depression in their lives testify to the huge help and encouragement that the Psalms have been to them.

The first encouragement to take from the Psalms is that, contained within these God-breathed words, are deep emotions, deep negative emotions. This deals head-on with the common misconception that the life of a believer is one of happy immunity from the emotional pain that life brings. The psalmists speak of the joy of knowing God to be sure, but also of their extreme anguish, fear and confusion in the face of suffering (whether suffering with a clear cause such as opposition, isolation or guilt, or sometimes no recorded cause at all). They do not just sail through these difficulties with unshaken serenity or care-free optimism. They often express real hope, peace and joy in the midst of trial, but rarely without telling also of their emotional torment.

Psalm 6, for example, may end on a confident note, expecting victory over enemies, but in the meantime, the writer's soul is in 'anguish' crying out, 'How long O Lord, how long?' Indeed, he is 'worn out with groaning', 'weak with sorrow', his couch is soaked through from his weeping. Here is no 'stiff upper lip' response to his painful circumstances.

God can cope with such extreme emotion as we wait for him to deliver us, in this life or in the next. Such 'groaning' is simply part and parcel of life this side of the new creation, where God will wonderfully wipe away every tear. Depression is part of the groaning of this life. But it can be used to loosen our grip on this world, and help us to long, as the psalmist does, to be with our God more than we might in easier times.

Being depressed (or even just feeling low) is not then in itself, something to hide from God or to be ashamed of. God knows that it is a natural part of this fallen life and he himself groans for us to know that restoration we long for and have been redeemed for (see Rom. 8:18-27). Who better, then, to turn to in the midst of suffering?

IN THE DEPTHS OF DARKNESS

In Psalm 88 the writer is 'in the lowest pit, in the darkest depths'. We aren't told why, but he is a desperate man, his 'soul is full of trouble'. He feels intensely isolated, a million miles from his God, whom he blames for his troubles. It seems to him that God has rejected him and let him be overwhelmed with sorrow. Indeed, he ends by saying that not God, but 'the *darkness* is my closest friend'. Hardly the confident note of hope that many other psalms about suffering end on.

We may wince at his lack of 'faith' perhaps, after all language like that doesn't sound very 'Christian'. If he were a friend of ours we might think he was rather self-absorbed with a very poor grasp of God's promises, his theology badly distorted.

But, at times, depressed believers will also feel closer to the darkness than to God who, from their vantage point, seems to have abandoned them. For them, this apparently bleak psalm can be a great comfort. The psalmist's experience is given for us to learn from. For what we see is a man of faith. His view of God may be distorted through his overwhelming emotion, his outlook on life may lack the perspective and joyful confidence that faith in Christ can give, but nevertheless it is still God to whom he is turning. And he is being utterly real before him. He is pouring out his heart to God, even though no easy answers or speedy assurances seem to come.

It can be very hard to keep praying through the depths of depression. But the example of this afflicted psalmist (much like the example of Job) reminds us that God wants to hear honest prayers in such times. He is not interested in us sorting out the anger and accusations we may feel towards him first. How can we deal with such feelings without his help anyway? He is the place to turn, and he alone, whatever state of mind we are in. It is better to pray real, honest, even angry prayers than not to pray at all. Prayer recognises God is still God.

CLINGING ON TO HOPE

In the pair of Psalms 42–43, we find the psalmist away from Jerusalem (and therefore away from God's symbolic presence), experiencing some kind of oppression. Unsurprisingly his soul is 'downcast' and he longs for his God. The psalmist is not suffering with depression per se (although Ps. 42 43 are often used in talks on the subject of depression). He is more likely to be suffering grief over his loss of Jerusalem. Yet in his grief he is displaying several of the symptoms that those who are depressed will recognise.

Emotionally, he can't stop crying, he is downcast, disturbed, overwhelmed. Physically, his whole body aches. Indeed many psalmists record physical symptoms such as pain, sleep loss and appetite loss associated with severe emotional pain (for example, Ps. 32, 38, 102) and such physical symptoms are frequently present in depression.

Spiritually, he feels God has forgotten him and is beyond his reach. This feeling of being rejected by God who now seems to be a million miles away is very normal for the depressed believer and for the psalmists. It is not reality, but it feels like it.

Mentally, it is interesting to notice how he feels about how he is feeling – he is bewildered by it! He knows that it doesn't make logical sense, 'why are you so downcast?' And yet he simply is downcast, and feels pretty helpless and overcome by it all.

There is much to be learnt from this psalmist in terms of handling our emotions when they seem to be getting the better of us. It is encouraging to see him along with so many other psalmists, pouring out his heart honestly before God. He asks God questions, he doesn't bottle up his pain and confusion – rather he directs his honest thoughts God-ward. And though he accuses God of forgetting him, yet his faith shines through as he asks this same God to help him.

The psalmist also 'preaches to himself'. He tries to stand back from himself and point a few things out to his soul, letting the objective truth he has been taught about God, speak to the subjective feelings that cause him to question God. He tells himself to put his hope in God, suggesting that it doesn't come naturally to him to do that, it takes conscious decision. And, as he does so, hope reappears, 'I will yet praise him, my Saviour and my God'.

It is very hard to feel at all positive about the future when depressed. Yet here, though he feels no joy at the moment, the psalmist holds onto the hope that God will somehow bring him back to that place of praise once again. He doesn't know when or how, but he is clinging to the character and promises of God who is his Saviour and his God.

Such confidence won through preaching to one's soul, won't always be the experience of the depressed believer. It is very unlikely to be the case for those who are in the very depths of depression, where the dark sentiments of Psalm 88 can be better related to. Yet, in the glimmers, as the depressed believer begins to crawl out of those depths, it is feeding truth to the soul that will strengthen it to hope, and to pray, and to trust.

TRUSTING GOD'S FINAL WORD

It is a beautiful thing that in the Psalms people's words to God become God's words to us. So much does God understand and treasure our human experience, even the depths of pain. He remembers our sufferings, storing 'our tears in a bottle' (Ps. 56:8) – he contains it all and no experience we go through is beyond his knowledge, his love or his power. And this is good news, because it means even the darkness cannot hide us from him (Ps. 139:11-12).

Above all, the Psalms point us to God's ultimate Word to us: His Son, the Lord Jesus. During his life on Earth, Jesus quoted the Psalms on numerous occasions showing he himself was the fulfilment of all they spoke of. He was the true Son of Man, the true Anointed One, the true King. But he was also the true forsaken man. He quoted the beginning of Psalm 22 as he hung in anguish on the cross: 'My God, my God, why have you forsaken me?' His experience of our humanness reached its climax in the absolute depths of despair. He received the terrible punishment for our sins in the agony of being cut off from God. Not only does this mean salvation for us as we trust in his amazing sacrifice on the cross, but also it means that there is no level of human pain and rejection that Jesus has not personally experienced. It means that in him we have a Great High Priest who is able to sympathise with our weaknesses, who has a throne of grace, not of condemnation. And wonderfully it means we can actually approach this throne with confidence to find grace and mercy to help us in our time of need (Heb. 4:14-16).

Trusting God in the darkness:
Using what God has provided

6

Trusting God in the darkness:

Using what God has provided

So how do we get through depression and stay believing? By the grace of God, quite literally! Above all it is his sovereign grace that holds on to us, not our ability to hold onto him. But part of his holding onto to us is through the 'means of grace' he has provided. None of these things are rocket science, no special techniques, just the normal things we do to keep going as Christians.

PRAYER
Be real. Come to God as you are rather than trying to sort yourself out first. Pour it all out to him and ask him to help you. And be realistic, praying when you can,

with others or for short periods of time if lacking energy or concentration. Prayer is the most important thing – if we let the lines of communication go down we will feel further and further from God and less inclined to trust him or seek his help. Giving thanks (for anything!) keeps us mindful of God's goodness and is a way to express our joy in Christ even when we don't feel it. Confessing specific sin is also important to keep doing, but this is not in order to perpetuate unbiblical feelings of guilt. We need to remember the cross secures our forgiveness however guilty we may feel – grace has the last word. Keep giving thanks for that!

Bible

The Bible is the best self-help manual we have! We use it to help us keep our eyes on God, to 'preach the gospel to ourselves', hope in the promises and identify and correct any wrong thinking. With the lack of energy associated with depression we need to make it easy, so go to passages that are easily accessible, use Bible reading notes, write verses on cards/post it notes, read the Bible with someone else, listen to sermon tapes, listen to Christian music – whatever it takes to remind us of the truth which sheds light in the darkness. Some people find it helpful to keep a record of what God has been teaching them and record verses that have touched them in a notebook. It is important to have realistic expectations of Bible reading and it may be the last thing you want to do. But to try to keep doing it every day, even though there are no feelings, will be the eventual path to recovery. As with prayer, it is much harder to start doing it again once we have stopped.

FELLOWSHIP

God has provided us as a family to share one another's burdens. Keep talking to Christian friends or an older Christian and going to church/small group. If this is difficult, ask others to go with you. Depressed Christians often feel like they have nothing to give and are simply useless to God, so it's helpful to keep serving in any practical ways appropriate. This also helps us to be outward looking when depression can make us very introspective. It's important to make church leaders/pastors aware of your struggles – they may have helpful suggestions or could point you to an older Christian who could help. Indeed, the church family should be the most natural place to seek support, before professional counsellors. There may be many good reasons why the severely depressed Christian should seek a form of professional talking treatment. However, if it is simply needing someone they can talk to, then ideally this is an activity fundamental to being part of God's family: caring for one another and encouraging one another in Christ.

MAKE THE MOST OF PRACTICAL ADVICE AND COMMON SENSE

We are not just spiritual and emotional beings. We have physical needs, which, if not met, can have consequences for our mental health. Make sure you eat and drink properly, get plenty of rest, take time off if you need to, get exercise and fresh air. It's important to have only small, manageable goals for each day (perhaps writing a letter, clearing up a room, making a meal, meeting a friend), and to keep thinking short term to avoid taking on any more worry than the day ahead.

We are also deeply social beings, so seek support from friends and family where possible. Being with other people may be the last thing we feel like doing if we are depressed, but it provides distraction and keeps us from too much self-absorption. Friends can also help us to avoid unhelpful behaviour that may sometimes accompany depression, such as personal neglect, overeating, overspending or drinking. They can also aid with the daily tasks that just might seem too much some days, like shopping or getting the children off to school.

SEEK MEDICAL HELP IF APPROPRIATE

If the depression persists or is getting pretty bad, or if it helps just for peace of mind, go to the doctor. If prescribed, don't worry too much about taking antidepressants. It may be helpful to think of them as a mental/emotional plaster cast. Just as one would put a leg in plaster for the healing of the broken bone to begin and to allow normal functioning in the early stages of that healing, antidepressants allow someone to regain some mental control and balance, some emotional 'breathing space' to think clearly about the issues and plan how to make progress. Similarly, if recommended you could try CBT or another form of counselling (and meet regularly with a mature Christian who you can chat the treatment through with). A big barrier for many people in getting help for their depression is the stigma attached to mental illness and this can prevent people from acknowledging their depression and seeking the help they may need. This may be a particular issue for Christians who think that as Christians they ought not to feel depressed. It can also be tempting for Christians to think that they should be able to cope with their illness without needing to resort to medical help. Whilst this may seem admirable, in some respects it is also foolish. As Christians we would not usually refuse to have conventional treatments for physical illnesses and we should not see illnesses such as depression any differently. We should encourage depressed Christians to seek medical help – and to see it not as an acceptance of defeat, but a wise approach to using all the resources God gives us to help us in times of difficulty.

James' story (43, Church Minister)

A few years ago I took my emotional vital signs and realised I was in a mess. I saw the family doctor who signed me off with stress and depression. Funnily enough things got worse rather than better before improving enough for me to return to work after five months. I stayed on antidepressants for three years.

This was a formative experience for me but, at the time, gruesome and excruciating. Not only was I basically very low but I had mood swings, a distorted, even slightly paranoid outlook, and other symptoms. I know that I became very difficult to live with. My wife was very patient but at times she needed a break.

Spiritually, I made some good choices and bad choices. A good choice was to read a bit of the Bible and pray the Lord's Prayer out loud every day. It took less than two minutes. Some days I was numb. Other days none of it felt very meaningful. But I would have been worse without it. I also turned to bits of Scripture by depressed people like Psalm 13 and Jeremiah 20. They were oddly comforting.

A bad choice was to become patchy in my church attendance. It was complicated for me as a minister. But it would have been better to have come late and left early at my church or another one than to try to go it alone.

It was important for me to see the family doctor and to have both medication and counselling. The medication calmed me down, helped the sleeping and lifted my mood a bit. The skill and sympathy of the counsellors made it easier to explore some of the roots of the breakdown and to cope with the difficulties of the immediate situation. I had two friends who met with me (separately) more or less weekly: their gift to me was that they listened without trying to fix me. It was hard when people did try to fix me, especially if the solutions were simplistic. What I needed were folk who were ready to share the load with me a little rather than run away from it.

Overall I am kind of glad it happened. I learned a lot about myself. I can help others a bit better. I learned a lot about God too. I am not free from depression or anxiety now but I am better equipped to cope with my vulnerability. The insights, techniques and self-care I have learned are invaluable. And it has all come together in Christ, whom I have learned to trust more.

Helping the
depressed

7

7

Helping the depressed

For those who are involved with helping a depressed person, this can sometimes seem almost as overwhelming and all-consuming as the depression itself. Being on the outside of a loved one's depression can lead to real feelings of helplessness, frustration and anxiety as to the best way to help. There is rarely a simple way forward in helping someone else deal with what is essentially such a personal struggle, but the following give some ideas on actions and attitudes that can help, and that can hinder. In the appendix on pastoral care, Ed Shaw, Assistant Minister at Emmanuel, Bristol, UK gives a personal perspective on his experiences of pastoring those suffering from depression.

ATTITUDES AND ACTIONS TO AVOID

• JUDGING

It is very easy to judge, withhold sympathy or get frustrated with people who are depressed and to assume (especially for Christians) that it is a spiritual problem resulting from an ungodly attitude or sinful behaviour. This is exactly what Job's friends thought and God condemned their assumptions in the strongest terms. We just do not know all the factors contributing to someone's depression. We cannot understand their specific struggles, their God-given temperaments and emotional make-up, their personal circumstances, the effect of their own history, medical problems and so on. Nor do we know why God has allowed this in their lives, or how he might use it. So we need to be very slow to assume anything, and even slower to assume that we would handle things better if it were us.

• BEING TOO QUICK TO SUGGEST CAUSE OR SOLUTION

We must also avoid doing too much analysing for them. It is tempting to offer a complete diagnosis of the problem, quickly followed by a solution package. But we would do better to be slow to speak and quick to listen. Instead of telling them what we think God must be teaching them, we need to trust that God himself is ministering to them and that their growth and recovery can happen according to his timescale and agenda, not ours. We need to restrain our solution mentality if that is our tendency, and be humble in how we talk and listen.

- FEELING INADEQUATE TO HELP

On the other hand, sometimes we can go to the other extreme and assume that we have nothing to offer. Perhaps God has given us a personality and circumstances which mean we can be fairly even-keel about life, or even generally up-beat, and we can't relate to depression at all. This can cause us to fall into the previous two traps, or it can paralyse us into having no confidence to do anything. But God has given us each other, and told us to teach, admonish, comfort and encourage each other. All this means speaking. We do need to do a lot of listening, but there is a vital place for words. Gentle, sympathetic, kind words, but also words that question wrong thinking about themselves or about God or about their circumstances. Also words of constructive advice, of praise and of encouragement.

• MAKING THE PERSON YOUR PROJECT

We all love to be needed and it can be tempting for us when we have a friend who is depressed to let them become dependent on us. We can think, without even realising it, that we are going to be the answer to their problem, that without us they won't get through. Firstly, if we believe in God and his sufficiency, this simply isn't true. Secondly, although God may have a really important part for us to play in someone's growth and recovery, it will only be a part, and the likelihood is that others will also have a part. In fact it will be more healthy for the person and for you if several others do have a part in helping them through.

• TAKING ON MORE THAN YOU CAN BEAR

Whilst you will want to help a depressed friend or family member as much as possible, there can be times when it becomes very hard, perhaps too hard. It may be helpful to remember that you are the person's friend, but not their doctor or their therapist. Again, involving others in supporting the depressed friend will help to ease the burden.

WAYS TO HELP

- PRAY

This is surely the most important thing! It acknowledges that God is in control and can keep and change the depressed person. And tell them you are praying for them – that is one of the most encouraging things to hear.

- LISTEN

Really try to understand how they are feeling so that what we say is more likely to be appropriate. Also don't underestimate the loving value of just listening – that's why non-directive counselling is so popular!

- GIVE PRACTICAL ADVICE AND SUPPORT

Give practical advice about common sense lifestyle measures such as getting regular exercise and having a good daily routine including a healthy pattern for going to bed and getting up. It may also be appropriate to challenge the depressed person if some of their behaviours may be making the situation worse – for example drinking too much alcohol. Give practical support in helping them to do these things – cooking a meal with them, going for a walk, helping them to do practical jobs that need doing, such as sorting out their finances or doing their washing. Go to church with them as often it is very hard for a depressed Christian to face other believers. A specific practical action that may be helpful is offering to go with the person to their appointment with a doctor or therapist – in part this is to help them to keep the appointment, but also because some company in the waiting room is a good support. If the depressed person finds it hard to talk about their situation then a friend who can help them explain things to the doctor or therapist may be a great help – but sometimes it may be better to stay out of the actual meeting and just wait in the waiting room.

- PRAISE AND ENCOURAGEMENT

One of the most difficult things about being depressed is the feeling of having failed and like you are never going to get out of it. Praising someone for the tiniest signs of progress, even if it is just that they got through a morning with people without withdrawing, can remind them that progress is possible. It also shows that you haven't rejected them but have high hopes that they will get through and are not condemned to 'failure'. Especially encourage them in any signs that they are holding on to the promises of God, however weakly.

- REASSURE WITH THE TRUTH

A timely verse can be such an encouragement for the depressed believer – even the simplest truths that God is compassionate and good and is in complete control, that Jesus died for them and they are spotless before him, that one day there will be no more tears when we are with the Lord, and so on. Remember they will be so vulnerable to believing lies at the moment and need to hear truth, gently and lovingly applied. And repeatedly applied, even if it doesn't seem to be sinking in. The absence of hearing simple gospel truths could mean they spiral down into believing the lies. Don't be insensitive though – shoving verses at people without showing that you completely sympathise with the pain they are feeling can do more harm than good.

- HELP TO IDENTIFY WRONG THINKING

There will be a place, although perhaps not in the early or most painful stages of depression, to gently challenge any seriously wrong thinking or behaving. Some depression can actually be caused by sinful attitudes such as unwillingness to forgive or behaviours such as an addiction that the person won't give up. This needs to be challenged by showing that God's will for their life is better than that, and that through repentance and obediently trusting God's way of thinking and behaving they can know his presence and blessing even in painful circumstances. But for most believers who are depressed the wrong thoughts such as 'God has it in for me' seem to be more the result of the depression. These can be questioned after time if they are still being held on to, but it is really important to remember most of the time it really is just the depression talking. Most believers will not be saying such things when the depression has lifted and they can think clearly. After all, remember that Job said some pretty outrageous things about God when he was in the depths!

- SEEK SUPPORT YOURSELF

It can be extremely draining looking after someone who is depressed and the depressed person probably won't realise just how much, because it is especially hard for them to look out of themselves at the moment. Having others you can talk things through and pray with is helpful, but avoid using that to betray confidences or to grumble about the depressed friend.

• PERSEVERE

Proverbs says that a 'friend loves at all times' (Prov. 17:17). Few things test friendship like depression. There can be an awful lot of give and not much take. Try to remember that with most people who are depressed this is only for a season, and there may be a time when the roles are reversed. Treat them how you would want to be treated. They will be terrified of rejection at this time so be sensitive and stick with them. It is more blessed to give than to receive, and indeed this is how Jesus treats us – he doesn't forsake us or give up on us, weak as we are. He is the friend that sticks closer than a brother and we are blessed when we imitate him.

HELPING UNBELIEVERS

There may be little difference on a practical level between the way we might seek to help a Christian and a non-Christian. Our human needs are the same and, as we have seen, a lot of the help needed is not necessarily directly 'spiritual', just as depression is not usually an entirely spiritual problem.

Helping depressed friends who don't know Christ is a great way to show them the love we have received in him, and reflecting the character of our God who is good to all that he has made. We need to be careful we aren't using our position of caring for such friends simply in order to 'convert' them. Our love is to be genuine and not manipulative.

Having said that, if we love them we will long for them to know Christ! And it is certainly true that when people are brought very low, they can be more open to asking the big questions of life that get pushed under the carpet when life is going well. Many Christians can testify that God used suffering, including depression, to bring them to put their trust in him.

Turning to Christ is unlikely to mean the depression disappears over night, but clearly it changes the most important thing – our relationship with our Maker, bringing new life and making real change now possible. So opportunities to point depressed unbelievers to the forgiveness and hope we can have in Christ should not be passed up! But all pressure should be avoided, remembering that the depressed person is a vulnerable person, with the potential to make a profession of faith that is not about a real surrendering to Christ as Lord, but simply an emotional desperation for something 'out there' to make things better. Time, unconditional love and acceptance and above all, prayer, will be needed in order to tell the difference.

Appendix 1
Struggles with Depression:
A personal point of view[1]

ROGER CARSWELL,
Yorkshire-based evangelist

I am not a doctor, psychologist or psychiatrist, but I have been a patient. What I share is simply one person's journey with depression, but I do not pretend to be a medical expert or understand the workings of the mind. However, like every other individual, including medical workers themselves, I battle against human frailty of one sort or another. For some people that may mean the limitation of physical weakness, for others it

---

1   This article first appeared in 'Where is God in a messed up world?' Roger Carswell (IVP 2006)

can be emotional or mental hurdles that may seem insurmountable.

I understand depression to be when the inward mental and emotional structure that normally supports our human existence, weakens, crumbles or becomes distorted. Levels of depression vary from mild mood changes, to clinical depression or manic depression, with its 'ups' and its 'downs'. Depression can be triggered by a crisis, or develop in the mind of someone who otherwise appears to be well and in control of life. When I was depressed it was hard to remember what it felt like to be well, and now I am well, it is difficult to recall just how it felt to be sick.

What I have been through is a common enough experience, though it is nothing compared with those who suffer from manic depression. Charles Spurgeon suffered depression after seven people died in a stampede when someone cried out 'fire' in one of his crowded worship services. William Cowper, who suffered from manic depression, attempted suicide for the third time the day after he wrote the hymn 'God moves in a mysterious way'. Elijah,

Jeremiah, David and Job were familiar with the struggles of depression.

PERSONAL EXPERIENCE

Converted at the age of fifteen, I have always regarded myself as a fairly cheerful character. However, I recall talking with a pastor concerning depression when I was just sixteen, and busily involved in the Lord's work on a beach mission in the sunny summer. Clearly, there has been an issue with depression within me for a long time. As well, from teenage years, I have been an intermittent insomniac, who works late nights, but then finds it difficult to sleep. I love my work as an evangelist, and can be a workaholic. I don't find it easy to 'switch off' or rest, and rarely have a break. And then, speaking personally, I can be a sensitive soul who feels deeply for the hurts of others, and it is not easy to shake off the thoughts of what others are suffering. I take these things to heart, and they remain there gnawing away at me.

Four or five years ago, I began to find certain aspects of my work overwhelming. Every phone call, and we have three lines coming into our home, seemed too much for me; it became increasingly hard for me to stay in other people's homes when away on missions. I couldn't cope with inconsequential chatter, or even the laughter of others. I became annoyed even when people asked me to preach somewhere (which, of course, is my life's work!) wishing people would just leave me alone.

I searched my own heart to see if there was any sin to which I was clinging that was coming between the Lord and me. Whilst not claiming to be sinless, I sincerely believed that all my sins were 'under the blood' and that there was nothing hindering my relationship with the Lord. Jesus had died paying the penalty of my wrong doing, and I was trusting in the crucified, now risen Christ as my Lord and Saviour. I loved Him with all my heart and longed to see others coming to a saving faith in Jesus, too.

A doctor friend talked with me, and advised me to take a Sabbatical, and so I set about cancelling various future appointments to give myself a four-month break. (Looking back, that period became sick leave rather than a Sabbatical). By the time that the four-month period had arrived, my state of mind had deteriorated.

I was beginning to sink into a depth of great, inward darkness. I did not want to talk with anyone. I continued to regularly have my devotions and go to church, but avoided meeting with people at the end of the service.

My mind was telling me things that were not true. For some time, I had thought I would collapse whilst preaching in the pulpit. I believed nobody cared whether I lived or died. I went to bed each evening hoping I would die in the night, and woke up the next day feeling I could not face the hours ahead. However, I never doubted God, even in my lowest moments. I was convinced that God was in control of all that was going on, and that He would not waste any experience I was having.

As well as talking with my very understanding family doctor, I went to a psychologist, who felt that if I could learn to breathe more slowly and take life more gently I would be better. My family doctor was keen for me to see a Counsellor, but I did not want to talk to anyone else. To suffer alone was itself too much for me, without the added burden of speaking to someone I did not know.

Many people wrote or sent cards assuring me of their prayers, each of which was appreciated. Two friends in particular, wrote at length, and one (helpfully) insisted on visiting me. Both assured me that I would eventually come through the depression. Although I felt there was no future, the fact that two people wrote the same thing, giving a more positive view of the future was very encouraging. I had yet to learn that today is not forever. I remember how on one occasion my son simply put his arm around me when he found me crying in my study. It was a moment of great comfort to me. Being hugged is part of being healed.

There were other Christians who hurt with their glib comments, such as 'Snap out of it' (I would have given my right arm to have been able to do that!), or 'Been there, done that'. Each one hurt, but no doubt they meant well. For me their comments led to more tears. God never spoke to my heart through them, or in that way.

SUICIDE?
Thoughts of dying dominated my mind. There was a craving for death. I knew that suicide is always wrong. It is a breaking of God's commandment, for God who

is the giver of life says we are not to take life, even our own. As well, it transfers the pain to the innocent family members who are left. I knew also that it is not the unforgivable sin, and at one particularly low time, I meticulously planned my 'accidental death'. I didn't want to cause God's enemies to blaspheme His name, so I planned a suicide that I was sure would be recorded as accidental death. I cannot tell you how near I was to taking my own life, but refrained from doing so, because I felt it would scar the life of my wife and four children until their dying day. Perversely, minutes before the dreadful moment of 'death', I was sharing the gospel with an unsaved man and longing that he should trust Christ as Lord and Saviour.

Although basically I don't drink alcohol, I wanted to get drunk. I thought that if I was drunk, at least for an evening I would not feel the tangible, emotional pain that was within.

With the passage of many months I was beginning to recover. However, I went to see a Christian psychiatrist in London. I had already tried three different types of drugs, two of which proved of no help, and one of which did strange things to my mind, and, foolishly, I abruptly stopped taking. That caused further traumas to my mind. The psychiatrist said that I was sick, but that he could help me. He put me on an older type of drug, and gradually this seemed to work as it drew me out of my depression. As a Christian, I am sure it is not wrong to be on medication. The fall has wrecked our beings, and we can be affected physically and mentally. As I would not hesitate to take medication if I was physically sick, so I was relaxed to take medication for my mind.

Eventually ... slowly ... erratically ... I came out of depression.

SUFFERING AND GLORY

I am aware that, as we read in 1 Peter and elsewhere in the Bible, suffering and glory both characterise the Christian life. We like to think that if there is suffering there will be no glory, or vice versa, but both are promised in the Christian life. The Christian is not immune from normal sicknesses. We can be sure that God's grace is sufficient for us in every situation, and He is well able to heal, if that is His purpose. God never wastes any tears. He never wastes any pain.

So, what have I learnt through this period?

First, I learnt afresh to trust God in the darkness. Because my mind was telling me things that were not true, I sought to speak to my innermost being and remind myself of 'true truth'. This is what the Psalmist does in Psalm 42. For example, in verse 5 we read, 'Why are you downcast, O my soul? Why so disturbed within me? Put your hope in God, for I will yet praise Him, my Saviour and my God.' The Psalmist spoke truth to his soul, and questioned its disturbed state. I had to remind myself of God's love toward me, of how He has blessed and helped in the past, and of what He promises in the future. It was good to know that Jesus, who Himself was called 'the Man of Sorrows', cared and could cope.

Secondly, in Isaiah 45:3 we read that God says: 'I will give you the treasure of darkness, riches stored in secret places, so that you may know that I am the Lord, the God of Israel, who summons you by name.' In the darkness and despair of depression, as I felt I was sinking ever deeper, God gave treasures. I experienced God's love and tender, therapeutic care. I am certainly aware of my own vulnerability in a way I had not recognised before, and I believe I have a more compassionate view towards those who suffer mental illness. Before I was quite dispassionate towards mental weakness. Don't we all need to learn to have Christ-like compassion to those whose physical and mental strength has collapsed?

I am aware that depression could recur for me. Frankly, I would fear it happening and would not wish the inward darkness on anyone, but I am also aware that God works all things together for my good and His glory. He is God and is in control, and though the 'inward man may perish' God can renew and keep me.

> Days of darkness still may meet me
> Sorrow's path I oft may tread;
> But His presence still is with me,
> By His guiding hand I'm led.

Appendix 2
Coping with my wife's depression:
A husband's perspective

ANDREW (46, FULL TIME PASTOR)
My wife suffers from bipolar depression. I have also suffered with depression and our conditions interact with each other, which is complicated. In some ways coping with her bipolar condition is as hard as my own depressive illness. Here are some of the things I have learnt and found helpful over the years.

Be real about what is happening. When your spouse gets mental illness, there is a loss, a loss of the person at their best or just as they normally are. They may become withdrawn which means you have less warmth in your life. They may lack energy which deprives you of fun. Or you have to go to social activities on your own. Family meal-times may rely on you to keep things bubbling along.

The partner of a depressed person may become painfully lonely. The relationship seems thin. They may have little to give you and may need a lot from you. It can feel like an emotional black hole with a strong gravitational pull sapping your life and energy.

Realise that you will have to bear a load that is heavier than most you have ever born. It will make you want to fix the problem to make it go away. But almost certainly you can't do that, and you just have to listen and sympathise.

It is important to do what you can and also to share the load around. Enlist others to come and listen. Or just come and sit. Don't try to do everything. The carer's self-care is vital. Take breaks. Take time away. Exercise. Do fun things. Guilt-free. If you become overloaded you won't be as much use to them. Just because they are down, you don't have to mirror the mood. But you will tend to unless you watch it.

On the other hand, be careful if you are tempted to try to 'sort them out'. If it really is depression, you probably can't. Not by problem-solving conversations anyway. Encourage them to work with the family doctor and possibly a counsellor or church staff-member. Help them with what the professionals suggest.

Find someone wise and sympathetic to talk about how you are and how you are coping. Try a church friend or leader. Talk to them regularly and be honest about how hard it is.

A big danger is seeking comfort in the wrong places. It can start so innocently with a caring enquiry from a colleague of the opposite sex. Because the comfort is so one-way at home you respond rather eagerly. Before too long a dangerous closeness develops. I praise God that he has protected me from this through people who warned me against it. I pass the warning on. It is all too easy for affairs to begin this way.

Above all, seek for God in the situation. A loss in any area of life opens a door for more of him. More direct reliance on him. More personal appreciation of him. Talk to your pastor or a sympathetic Christian friend and pray with them. It is hard to read this, I know, but it really is a chance to know Jesus better.

Appendix 3

A Pastor's experience of helping someone with depression

ED SHAW,
ASSISTANT PASTOR OF EMMANUEL, BRISTOL.
Rob was a young leader I was discipling as a young pastor. He was a keen Christian who was using his wonderful musical gifts to serve our church family each Sunday. I was meeting up with him every week to look at a bit of the Bible together and pray it into our lives. As we did this he gradually opened up about his long-term struggle with depression and about three months into our friendship he disappeared into a major depressive episode during which he made a number of attempts on his life

(including one on a church weekend away).
Soon our weekly meetings were happening
in the local hospital's psychiatric wing.

Rob's struggle with depression is one
of the best things that ever happened to
me as a young pastor. Why? Because it
forced me to engage with a pastoral issue
that around 1 in 5 of church family members struggle with in some shape or form,
at some stage of their lives. Admittedly his
experience of depression was particularly
bad, but that meant I couldn't side-step
the issue as I might have been tempted to
otherwise. Then, off the back of the back
of a lot of thinking about depression, I've
worked harder than I ever had before at
making sure churches I've served are better at dealing with the whole host of other
major pastoral issues that are, like depression, regularly experienced, but rarely
talked about.

Through Rob, and since Rob, what les-
sons have I learnt about the pastoral care
of those struggling with depression? Well
I've learnt the importance of:

• OPENING UP THE BIBLE WITH THEM.
When Rob was seriously ill someone coun-
selled me against continuing to look at a bit

of the Bible together. I was told it would be too much, pastorally insensitive. I foolishly listened until one day my frustration with then not knowing what to say or do led me to read Psalms 42 and 43 with him. Rob was incredibly helped in discovering that some of his experiences were captured in God's Word. He, we, wept through reading those Psalms together and from then on regularly returned to them and other passages that both allowed him to put his feelings into words and then hear God speak His Word into his feelings.

- REMEMBERING THE HOPE OF HEAVEN.
I once found Rob after he'd taken a large overdose on a church weekend away – it was during a period when he'd made a number of attempts on his life. As I did what needed to be done, the thought that kept returning was 'It won't always be like this' driven by the wonderful truths of Revelation 21. That kept me going that awful evening and then was soon passed on to Rob to help keep him going too.

- ENCOURAGING PEOPLE TO TALK HONESTLY.
Rob was an amazing model of this – he told you what he was going through in an open

way that many (including me) wouldn't. He wasn't ashamed of his sufferings and was keen for others to learn through them. So as he was slowly recovering from a three month depressive episode it was his idea to have an evening at church where we briefed church family members about depression and what they could do to help church family members who were depressed. We included an incredibly helpful interview with Rob.

• PREPARING PEOPLE FOR SUFFERING.

Rob could cope better with his depression because he knew that suffering was part of the deal as a Christian. Others don't because they've never been taught that it is. Seeing that difference in responses has made me keen to keep preparing church family members for God's school of suffering in whatever shape or form it comes for them. So in preaching, testimonies, small groups, everyday conversation I'm encouraging people to talk about how God has used suffering in their lives for His glory. So many churches produce Christians who are surprised and shocked by suffering rather than expecting that it will be one of the ways their loving Father God makes them more and more like Jesus.

- INVOLVING OTHERS IN PASTORAL CARE.

I can remember lying in bed and hearing the phone ring at 1 in the morning. I knew it would be Rob because it had been Rob at a similar time a number of times over the last week. I knew that he'd probably just want a chat but I also knew that there was a possibility that he was ringing to tell me he'd just taken an overdose. But I didn't pick up because I couldn't – seeking to care for Rob alone had brought me to the very edge of burn out and I could take it no more. The next day Rob and I met up and agreed that the night time chats he sometimes needed could best happen with The Samaritans and then, with a group of his friends from church, we drew up a rota of who would be around at other times to provide the listening ear, the company that he desperately needed when things were at their worst.

- PUTTING MENTAL HEALTH CARE IN PLACE.

As a church we paid for Rob to have some professional counselling to see if that would help. I sat in on the first counselling session because otherwise Rob was refusing to go. His family doctor was given my number and – with Rob's permission – we talked once. Our city's mental health emergency response team were wonderful in providing the support that Rob needed to cope with life when out of hospital. We didn't try and go it alone but we didn't let Rob go it alone into the mental health system either.

• BEING A GOOD FRIEND.
I so often felt out of my depth with Rob – because most of the time I was. I stopped panicking when I realised that what he needed most of all was just a good friend to spend time with – especially when he was feeling suicidal. But what was it best to do in those times? Always talk about his feelings? That was just depressing (for both of us). Always read the Bible? That was impractical. Our eventual answer (after plenty of research) – Blackadder. We watched all four series and then started again. They are what sometimes helped most. I tried to claim them on expenses as a result...

• PREACHING ABOUT DEPRESSION.
Sometimes I've preached whole sermons on the subject, more often I regularly apply Bible passages to church family members struggling with it. Both help create a culture in which depression is not regarded as

an un-talked about sin but instead a fact of life which is not beyond God's redeeming grace. Every time I've done this I've relied on the help of those I know who struggle with depression – to check that what I'm planning to say is actually helpful. Every time I've done this I've had conversations with people who've been helped as a result.

- REMEMBERING GOD'S AGENDA.

God is in the business of making us more and more like Jesus and seeing depression as part of this, rather than the plan gone wrong, has been crucial. Depression, like all suffering, exposes things about people that the good times keep hidden and with Rob that highlighted issues that would have otherwise perhaps have taken years to come to the surface. Some of those issues were not appropriate to highlight whilst so much else was happening but some were crucial to notice and talk about to help him slowly recover.

- DEPENDING ON GOD.

The crucible of Rob's depressive episode was good for my prayer life. So often there was nothing I could do but pray which was so good for a pastor who so often does loads of other things rather than pray. And praying with Rob was an amazing taste of what true dependence on God often looks like – crying out to him in the midst of pain, desperately asking him to rescue you before it's too late.

So do you see why Rob's depression was one of the best things that ever happened to me as a young pastor? It taught me so much in a way that nothing else would have done so well.

The most recent time I caught up with Rob I shared the profound impact his experiences had on me and how, in a unexpected way, I am so grateful to God for them as a result. And, wonderfully, he joined me in praising God for the positive impact they have had – and continue to have – on his life too. We remembered a truth we had both often had to cling on to in the midst of them:

> 'And we know that in all things God works for the good of those who love him, who have been called according to his purpose.' (Rom. 8:28)

Helpful reading and Internet resources

This is a list of some of the resources that we, and Ed Shaw, author of Appendix 3, have found helpful – it is far from a complete list!

SECULAR

Gillian Butler and Tony Hope, *Manage Your Mind* (OUP, 2007)

Tim Cantopher, *Depressive Illness: The curse of the strong*, (Sheldon Press, 2006) – really helpful for those who are suffering with depression off the back of something equivalent to burnout.

Matthew Johnstone, *I Had a Black Dog*, (Robinson, 2007) – A comic-style book written by someone who has suffered with depression and particularly helpful because it is short on words – but very clear on the struggles of depression.

Matthew & Ainsley Johnstone, *Living with a Black Dog* (Robinson, 2008) – The equally helpful companion volume to *I Had a Black Dog* written to help those living alongside those with depression.

Kwame McKenzie, *Understanding Depression* (Family Doctor Publications Ltd, April 2009) – a small book published by the British Medical Association giving an overview of causes and types of depression as well as treatments and self-help approaches.

John Preston, *You Can Beat Depression*, Impact Publishers (US, 2004) – both give very helpful medical information and practical self-help exercises using the CBT approach.

The Royal College of Psychiatrists (UK) has leaflets on Depression and other mental health problems available on their website http://www.rcpsych.ac.uk/mentalhealthinfoforall.aspx

The Samaritans – a charitable organisation providing support for those in distress and despair, including a 24 hour phone line (08457 90 90 90 in the UK) and internet resources http://www.samaritans.org/

MIND http://www.mind.org.uk/ is a mental health charity based in England and Wales. They provide information and have local support groups and a wealth of other resources.

Mood Gym http://www.moodgym.anu.edu.au/welcome an Australian website providing free online CBT.

CHRISTIAN

Christopher Ash, *Out of the Storm* (IVP, 2004) – an excellent and readable study of Job's suffering which points to the God who is in loving control.

Kirsten Birkett, *The Essence of Psychology* (Matthias Media, 1999) – gives a helpful Christian analysis of counselling and psychotherapy.

Gauis Davies, *Genius, Grief and Grace* (CFP, 2005) – a collection of mini biographies of well known and greatly used Christians who suffered with depression.

Julian Hardyman, *Maximum Life* (IVP, 2009) – This book on living the whole of your life for God's glory includes a helpful autobiographical chapter on how to do that when you're depressed.

Michael Lawson, *D is for Depression: Spiritual, psychological and medical sources for healing depression* (CFP 2008) – This is a self-help book about getting better – a resource for those who suffer or who are close to someone who is depressed.

John Piper, *When the Darkness Will Not Lift* (IVP, 2007) – gives comfort and guidance in looking to God through suffering depression.

Alie Stibbe *Barefoot in the Kitchen: Bible readings and reflections for mothers* (BRF, 2004) – An honest account of a woman's struggle with postnatal depression and motherhood, with short bible readings for each day.

Howard Stone, *Depression and Hope* (Augsburg Fortress, 1998) – gives excellent pastoral insights for helping those who are depressed.

Joanna Swinney, *Through the Dark Woods: A young woman's journey out of depression* (Monarch, 2006) – A young woman's account of her battle with depression. In it she relates her story, but also covers helpful tools towards recovery and looks at how to help others with depression.

Paul David Tripp, *Instruments in the Redeemers Hands* (Evangelical Press, 2003) and Timothy S. Lane and Paul David Tripp *How People Change* (New Growth Press, 2008) – look at how we are called to minister to each other in God's family to help facilitate Biblical change in our lives.

Edward T Welch, *Depression: A Stubborn Darkness*, (Evangelical Press, 2008) – A resource from the Christian Counseling and Educational Foundation (www.ccef.org) that is excellent at putting depression in the wider theological context of what God is doing in his children's lives.

Chris Williams et al, *I'm Not Supposed to Feel Like This* (Hodder and Stoughton, 2002) – a helpful and practical self-help book that uses the CBT approach in a Christian context.

Chapter 5 'Depression' of Vaughan Roberts' *Battles Christian Face* , (Authentic Lifestyle, 2007) – an exposition of Psalms 42 and 43.

Chapter 8 'Pastoral Care' of Tim Chester and Steve Timmis, *Total Church*, (IVP, 2007) on the role of the Gospel in pastoral care.

CCEF (The Christian Counseling and Education Foundation) is a counselling and education ministry based in America with the aim of restoring Christ to counselling. A variety of useful resources are available on their website http://www.ccef.org/ including talks to download.

The Association of Christian Counsellors http://www.acc-uk.org/ provides contact details of Christian counsellors in the UK.

Other books available on this topic...

D is for depression.

Spiritual, psychological and medical
resources for healing depression

Michael Lawson

ISBN 978-1-84550-151-8

D is for Depression

Spiritual, psychological and medical sources for healing depression

MICHAEL LAWSON

Depression seems to be everywhere. You all know someone who suffers from it – you may yourself? It has become such a part of the psychological landscape that it can be met with cynicism, or indifference, which is a problem – because Depression does exist – and people suffering from it need help.

The concept of *D is for depression* is what makes it immensely valuable. It is a self-help book about getting better – a resource for those who suffer, or who are close to someone who does. The content of this book is to be trusted because it has already been translated and read across the world – appearing on university and theological college reading lists. It is substantially based upon Michael's earlier book, *Facing Depression*. A book widely used by individuals, churches and in the training of those seeking professional skills to help others.

There are not many books that deal credibly with depression from both a Biblical and medical scientific angle. The absence of either leaves you with a less than holistic guide. This is one of the best of such books.

Michael Lawson is the Archdeacon of Hampstead and trains church leaders in practical theology.

"This book is a celebration of God's grace..." **John Stott**

GENIUS, GRIEF & GRACE
A Doctor Looks at Suffering & Success
DR. GAIUS DAVIES

CASE STUDIES:
Martin Luther, John Bunyan, William Cowper, Lord Shaftesbury,
Christina Rossetti, Frances R. Havergal, Gerard Manley Hopkins,
Amy Carmichael, C.S. Lewis, J.B. Philips, Martyn Lloyd-Jones.

ISBN 978-1-84550-359-8

Genius, Grief & Grace

A Doctor looks at Suffering and Success

GAIUS DAVIES

Dr. Gaius Davies introduces us to Martin Luther, John Bunyan, William Cowper, Lord Shaftesbury, Gerard Manly Hopkins, Christina Rossetti, Amy Carmichael, J.B. Phillips, C.S. Lewis, Martyn Lloyd Jones and Frances Ridley Havergal.

After a brief biographical introduction to each person, he shows us how he or she all had their particular trial, and how grace operated in each of them. He is not afraid to show how anxiety, guilt, depression and doubt can be present in the finest of Christian lives, but also goes on to show how divine grace can transform human weakness.

Dr Gaius Davies, FRCPsych, M Phil, DPM, was a Consultant Psychiatrist at King's College Hospital, London. He is a well-respected author.

Christian Focus Publications

Our mission statement –

STAYING FAITHFUL

In dependence upon God we seek to impact the world through literature faithful to His infallible Word, the Bible. Our aim is to ensure that the Lord Jesus Christ is presented as the only hope to obtain forgiveness of sin, live a useful life and look forward to heaven with Him.

Our books are published in four imprints:

CHRISTIAN FOCUS

Popular works including biographies, commentaries, basic doctrine and Christian living.

CHRISTIAN HERITAGE

Books representing some of the best material from the rich heritage of the church.

MENTOR

Books written at a level suitable for Bible College and seminary students, pastors, and other serious readers. The imprint includes commentaries, doctrinal studies, examination of current issues and church history.

CF4•K

Children's books for quality Bible teaching and for all age groups: Sunday school curriculum, puzzle and activity books; personal and family devotional titles, biographies and inspirational stories – Because you are never too young to know Jesus!

Christian Focus Publications Ltd,
Geanies House, Fearn, Ross-shire,
IV20 1TW, Scotland, United Kingdom.
www.christianfocus.com